You are not alone.

WRITTEN & DESIGNED BY

GINA DOBMEIER

WRITTEN BY: GINA DOBMEIER
DESIGNED BY: GINA DOBMEIER
EDITED BY: DINA LASKOWSKI, MINDI LEATHAM, KRISTEN UTLEY

Library of Congress Control Number: 2020919343
ISBN: 978-1-7356672-0-1

Contact: I Am Crowned Project at info@GinaDobmeier.com.

To see more of Gina's inspiring work and products please visit www.ginadobmeier.com

1st Printing

WITH SPECIAL THANKS:

TO MY DAUGHTER ANNABELLE AND SON ETHAN. YOU OPENED MY HEART TO LIVE AND MY EYES TO SEE BEAUTY IN THE MIDST OF GRIEF.

TO THE MOST SUPPORTIVE AND MOST PRECIOUS GIFTS IN MY LIFE, MY HUSBAND, RYAN, AND DAUGHTER'S, CADENCE AND MYLEE. THE FOUR SIMPLE YET PROFOUND WORDS I WANT YOU TO KNOW IS..

You are not alone.

THANK YOU FOR GIVING ME THE SPACE TO CREATE AND FOR ALWAYS CHEERING ME ON IN ALL MY ONGOING IDEAS. YOU ALL TEACH ME MORE THAN YOU WILL EVER KNOW.

♥

MOM

You are not alone.

Our minds like to tell us that we are.

We all go through loss, change, pain, unforeseen circumstances that may feel haunting and paralyzing.

That is your path, your story.

Look

within.

The emotions that flare
up are meant to lead you
down the path of the
unknown.

You know, the questions
you have asked yourself a
million times:

Which way do I *go*?

_____

Who *am I*?

_____

Will I ever feel *normal* again?

_____

What *is* normal?

_____

Every question leads to
more and more questions.

Let them reveal the
layers from within that
deserve attention. When
given the attention with
love and grace, healing
can begin.

This path of the unknown
is where dreams are
birthed, where beauty
awakens and
lessons are learned.

It's where fear and faith
collide to introduce to you
a new version of who you
were created to be.

Trust Yourself

and

Trust the Process!

Believe.

Every step of the way has a meaning.

It's time to open your eyes to see and ears to hear the greatest story that is about to be written, by you.

Invite healing and hope
into your being.

Here is where you will find
a new kind of freedom from
within.

Here you will find hope to
unlock the dreams that live
on the inside of you.

You are not alone.

Give yourself

permission.

Permission to
grieve, cry, be
angry, yell,
fight, and ask
all the
questions...

Permission to
smile, to live in
ways that make
you come alive:

Do what makes
you happy and
follow the light
inside.

Laugh

Take pictures

Eat your favorite food

Take a trip

Listen to music

Go for a walk

Search for beauty in
the small things

Welcome change

Start a new hobby or
pick up an old one

Whatever doesn't fit,

let it go.

Give yourself

time.

When you give yourself
the time it takes for
your heart to heal, there
lies a gift.

The gift of becoming
whole.

Seek wise counsel,
know that there is no
right or wrong way to
grieve and heal. There is
no saying goodbye to
the imprints that have
been left on your heart.

Those imprints are a
part of you.

They are your story and
what makes you, you.

The imprints on your heart will teach and prepare you to love and grow stronger in ways you could never imagine.

You are *bold* in the *knowing*.

You are *brave* in the *becoming*.

You are *beautiful* in the *making*.

Your life is so
worth living.
Everything is
going to be
okay.

You are not alone.

You are held
by arms of

love.

A love that is so
strong and always
present. A love that
will illuminate your
soul to find hope
and beauty again,
but this time in a
new way.

Trust

and

Believe

Learn to become

still.

The stillness and silence allows
for readjusting and realigning of
the mind. It brings clarity.

Learn to enjoy the silence
and stillness. You will find
it serves a greater
purpose and meaning
within your process.

Quiet the noise.
Become curious.
Find the time.

It's easy to look at what's happening on the outside, but to stop and take notice of what's happening on the inside is what matters the most.

Search as though you are
on the greatest
adventure of your life.

Imagine you are going to go
off roading for a little while.

Get Messy.
Get Dirty.
Get Wild.
Seek the Thrill.
Live in Wonder.
Look Up and All around.

You will find your way back
to You.

When the taste of freedom comes, don't be afraid of it, don't question it, just savor it.

Become comfortable with the uncomfortable.

Freedom

is the very thing your mind and
body needs to keep moving
forward within becoming
whole.

There is purpose.
There is meaning.
There is more than what you
can taste, touch, feel, smell,
hear, and see right now.

And Remember...

You are not alone.

Photography Credit For

You are not alone

Page 8, Tirza VanDijk / unsplash.com
Page 14, Cinescope Creative / unsplash.com
Page 18, Alekon Pictures / unsplash.com
Page 23, Noah Silliman / unsplash.com
Page 26, Kunj Parekh / unsplash.com
Page 33, Henrique Macedo / unsplash.com
Page 38, Kate Chikina / unsplash.com
Page 40 Fabrice Villard / unsplash.com
Page 46, Leio McLaren / unsplash.com
Page 50, Jonathan Borda / unsplash.com

ABOUT THE AUTHOR

Gina Dobmeier is a wife, mom and founder of I Am Crowned Project. She wrote this book from her story after the loss of her stillborn Annabelle and late term miscarriage Ethan. Grief has been her greatest teacher and she wants you to know that you are not alone in the pain and trauma you endure. Gina discovered that there is beauty within pain, and that pain can be the very thing that awakens us to live from our true authentic self. Her desire is that as you read this book you find your path of healing to live from a place of wholeness and freedom.

What Once Was, is Now Crowned in Glory.

www.ingramcontent.com/pod-product-compliance
Lightning Source LLC
Chambersburg PA
CBHW071436040426
42445CB00012BA/1376